Just A Second

By: Courtney L. Edwards

ILLUSTRATED BY: KRYSTAL CARTER

Just A Second
© 2020 by Courtney L. Edwards
Illustrated by Krystal Carter

ISBN Hardcover:
978-0-578-77061-1

ISBN EBOOK:
978-1-0879-1416-9

Paperback ISBN:
978-0-578-80317- 3

my dedication

For my handsome son Keelan-Lee and
my beautiful niece Kahniya. You two inspire
me on a daily to continue!

Xoxo

CLE

One night as I lay Niya down, I kiss her goodnight and hug her tight.

Our normal routine. "Sweet dreams, see you in the morning."

SUPER GIRL

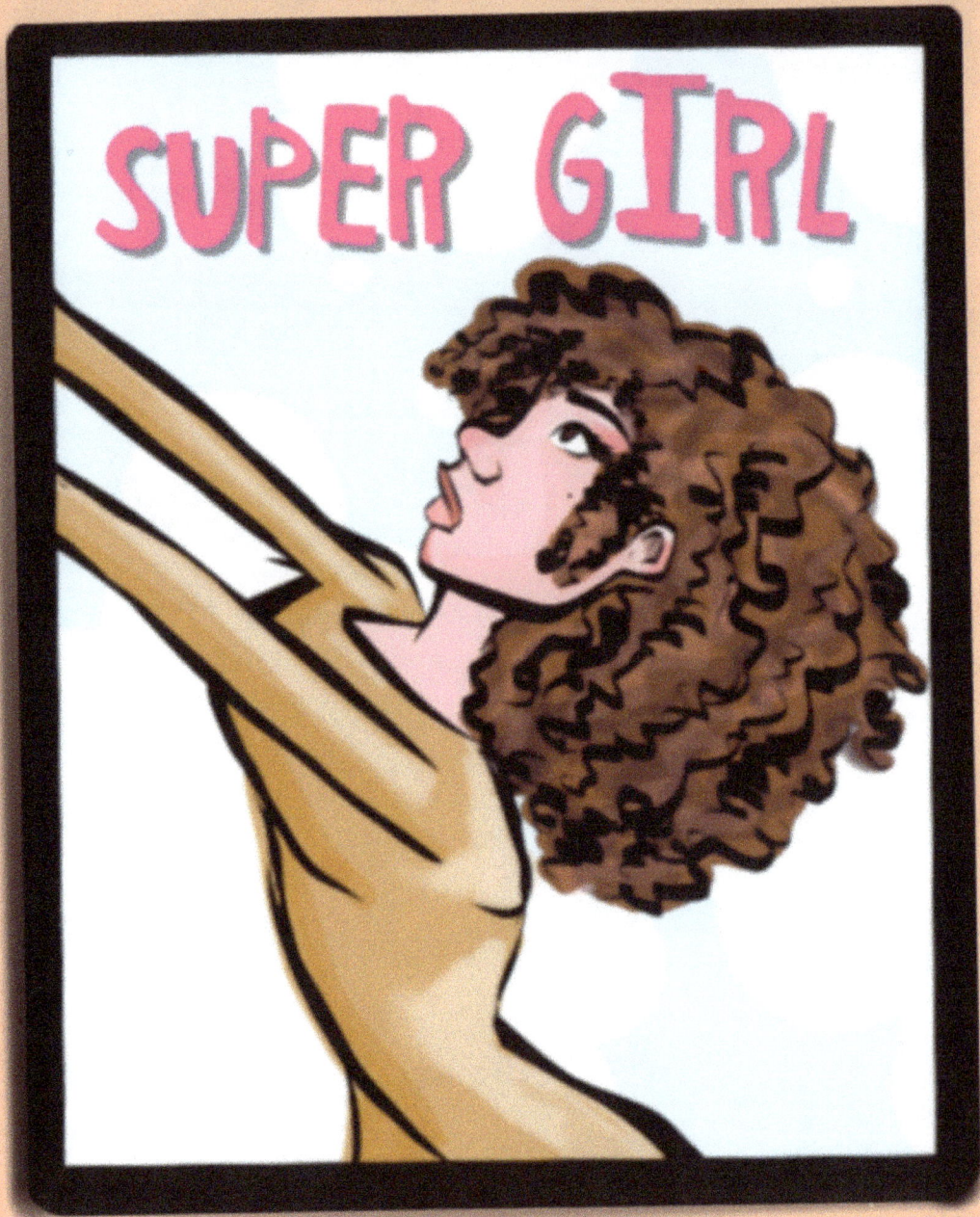

As I walk out, not hearing a sound,

she's standing
right behind me.

I giggle and say, "What are you doing?"

She says, "I want to watch a movie. You always watch movies, don't you?"

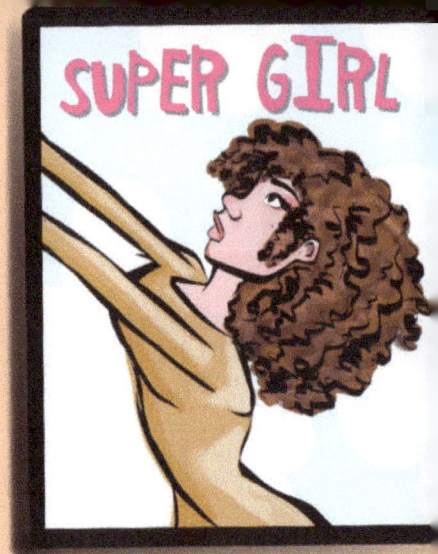

I grab her hand and place her back in bed.

I give her more kisses and hugs,
and I walk out.

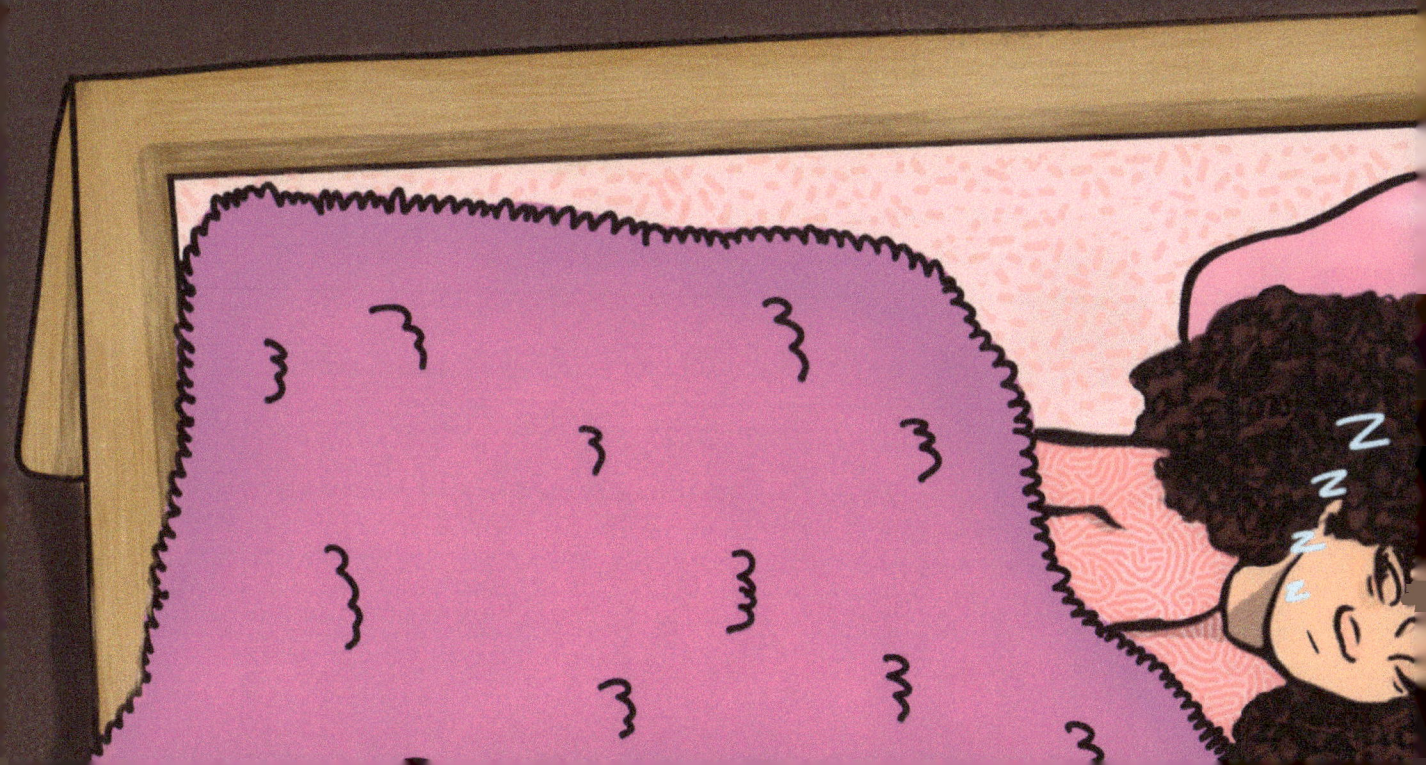

I was able to get to the bottom of the stairs, and then I look up. There she is! "OH MY GOODNESS, LITTLE GIRL, it is bedtime. Aren't you sleepy?" I ask her as I walk up the stairs to her.

She says, "No, Coco, I want to watch
a movie just for a second.

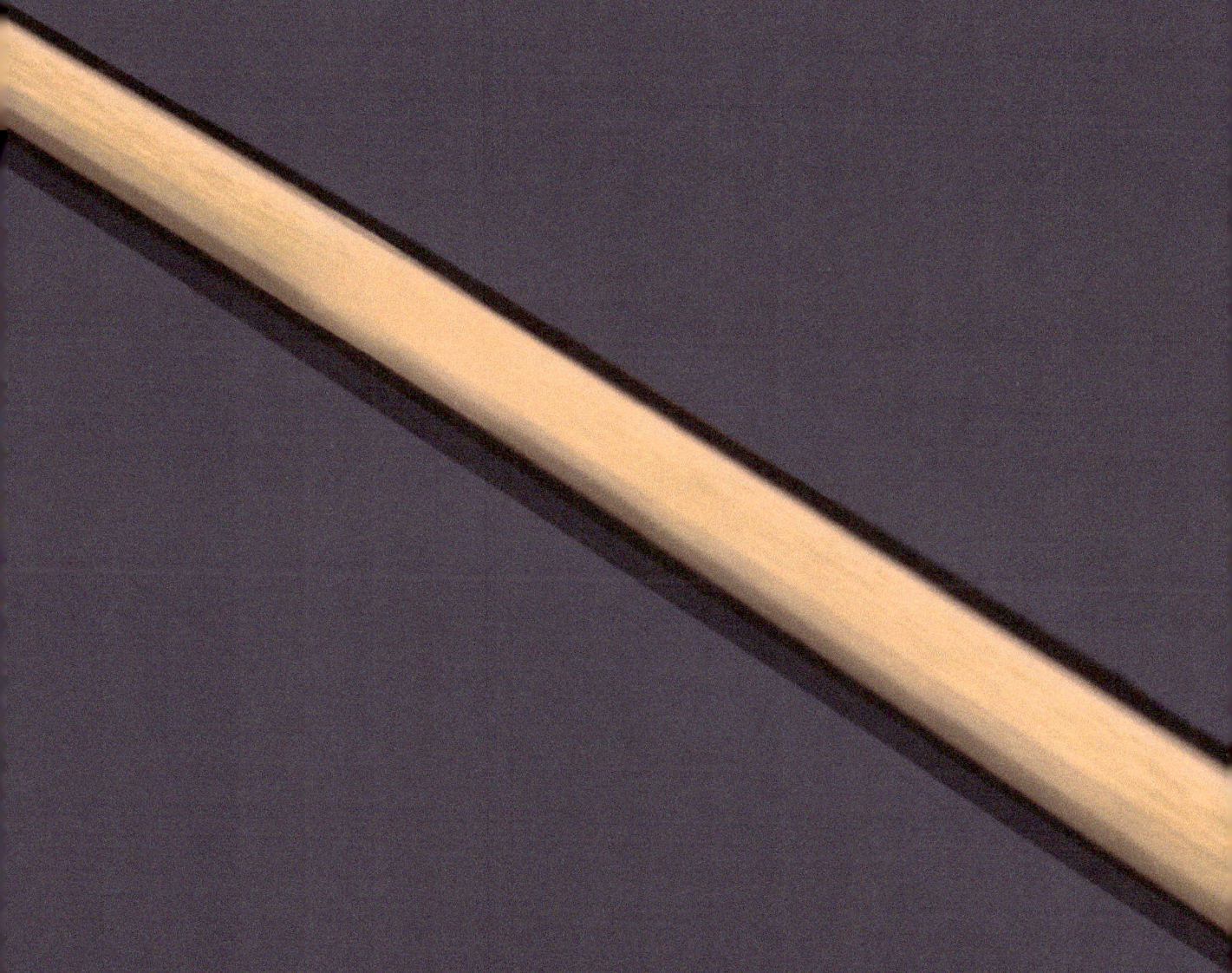

Just for a second?"

I gave in to that sweet little face. We go in my room, and I place a DVD on. I tell her, "You have to lay down and we're only watching for a second, then it's bedtime!"

She says, "Alright, Coco."

In my head I say, "lord, she's wide awake,

and lord, I'm
half asleep."

"If you're going to stay longer," I firmly stated. "You have to lay over there on that side, honey."

She said, "Can I have another pillow?"

"What? What is this? You can't have mine, and there's two on your side."

She says, "Ok, Coco."

I must have dozed off. I open my eyes quick and look over to her bright face and brown eyes watching the movie still. "Well, look at the time, baby girl. It's time to go upstairs."

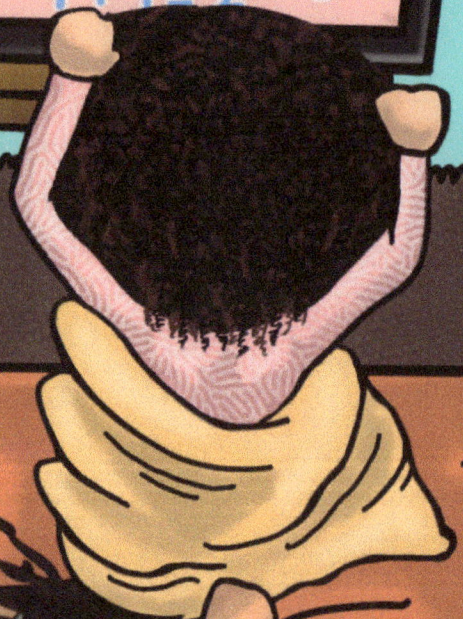

She said, "Just a second." A second,
we had plenty of seconds.

I picked her up this time and placed her in bed. She says, "CoCo, can you read to me?"

At this point, I crawled into her bed and said, "Baby girl, give aunty a second." (I was so tired. I had a long shift, and I have to work early tomorrow.)

Next thing you know, she had fallen asleep. In my head, I kept thinking of all the seconds/mins/hours I could have gotten real sleep, but it was all worth every second.

So, I walk out of the room to go get in my bed. I look up, and who's at the top of the stairs now? My son.

"Mommy, I don't feel good. Can you come up here for a second?"
"Just a second?"

Nicole

Thank you for not letting me take

this journey alone!

About the Author

Courtney L. Edwards is an author, philanthropist, fraternal twin and a California native. Courtney's passion for writing started at the age of 12. Writing has been her way of expressing herself when she was uncomfortable talking about personal things or adolescent topics.

She is a mother to a son with Autism Spectrum Disorder (ASD). Courtney vows to dedicate her time and energy to ensure her son has a normal life. Now she feels it's her time to be HEARD OUT LOUD! Courtney writes from her experiences and hopes that the readers can connect and relate to her. Courtney, who is also hearing impaired, has a true passion for giving back to the Greater Los Angeles Agency on Deafness Community. For more information, please visit courtneyledwards.com

The End

www.ingramcontent.com/pod-product-compliance
Lightning Source LLC
Chambersburg PA
CBHW040257100426
42811CB00011B/1291